Maxine - !

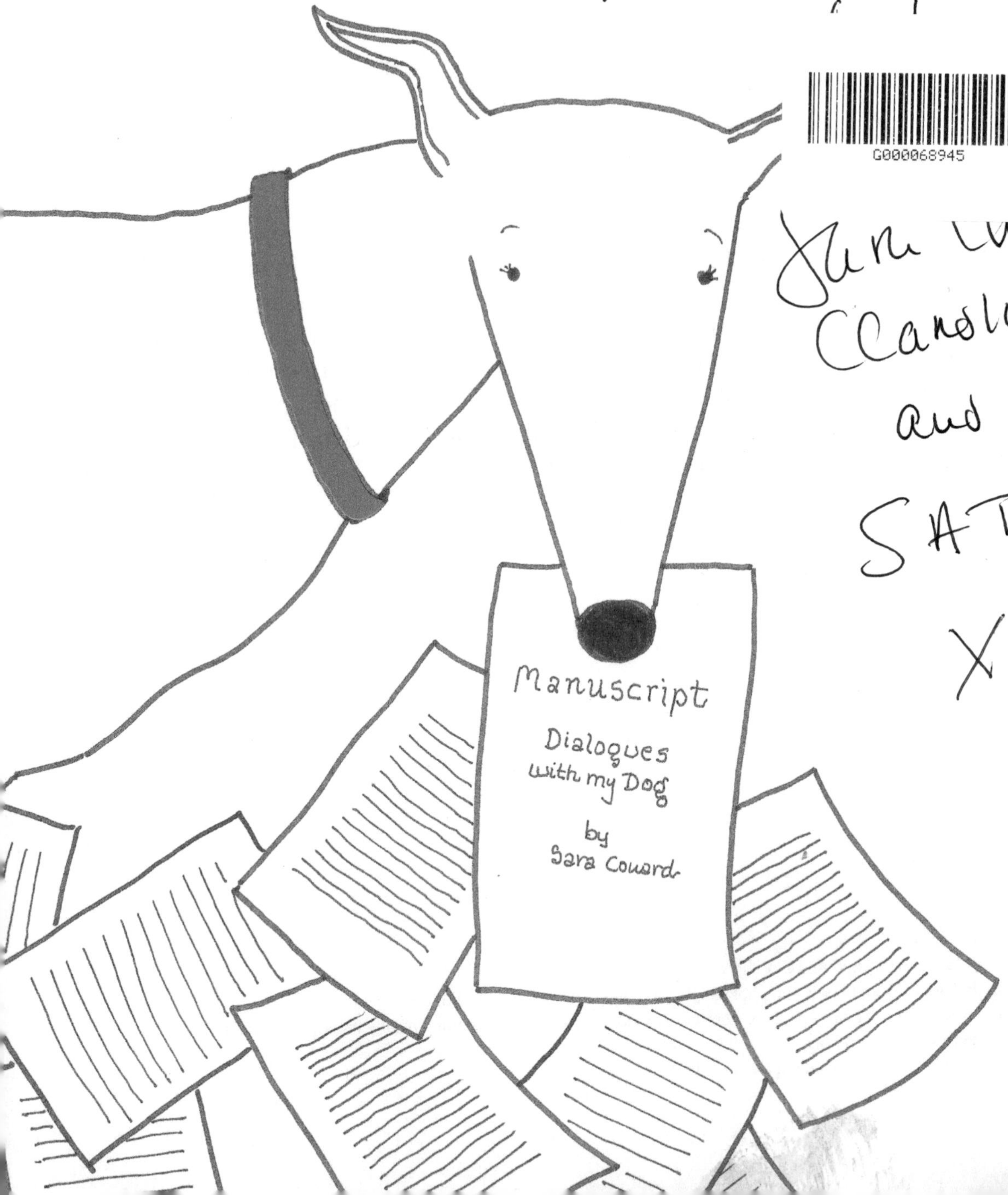
Manuscript
Dialogues with my Dog
by Sara Coward

(Caroline)
and
SATI
x

Dialogues with my Dog

This book is dedicated to the lovely Lynn Spooner, without whom I would never have met my dog, and never have written it.

This book wrote itself – I had no literary or financial aspirations in producing it. I just found myself sitting for minutes at a time, the conversations with my dog running through my head, and the incidents in our life together forming themselves into narrative. Finally, and after some resistance (I'm a lazy person) I decided it was time to bite the bullet and commit it to paper. I hope you'll enjoy it, finding it amusing and full-nosed but unpretentious, as they say of selected wines.

Every word is true. Thank you for reading!

Swift Publishing Ltd,
145-157, St John Street, London, EC1V 4PW
© Copyright Sara Coward (words and photographs) Ali Wylie (design and illustrations).
No part of this book may be reproduced, stored in a retrieval system, or transmitted by any means without the written permission of the author.
First published by Swift Publishing in October 2013
ISBN: 978-0-9568148-7-6

Programme

Curtain Raiser

The bedroom. Morning. Sati is curled up on the bed as usual;
he's a late riser. I leave the computer and sit beside him.

Me:
Sati, darling - I'm writing our story.

Sati:
(raising a metaphorical eyebrow)
Are you, Mother? Do I feature?

Me:
Feature? You're the main character!

Sati:
(only mildly impressed)
Oh. Good.

He buries his nose between his paws
and goes back to sleep.

Act One – Prologue

Since I was tiny, I've longed for a dog, and was never allowed to have one – in retrospect, a huge mistake on the part of my fastidious parents. I could have been a much happier child.

I should say at this point that I've always "done" voices for animals. I'm an actor, true, but this has nothing to do with performance. I started as a little girl, giving voices to my teddy bears and toy dogs (dolls never did it for me). It happens naturally and spontaneously, like breathing. I remember when I was a child there was a chap on television called Johnny Morris, who used to give animals voices. I never liked him much; it felt too contrived and self-conscious. But I've always found myself giving words to animals; I just look at them and discover I'm voicing their (projected) thoughts. It's an odd process, and many people hearing this must think I'm absolutely bananas. They may well be right. But there it is.

When I grew up and became independent, I shared my life with several real dogs and partners, most of whom lived very long and fulfilled lives. To the best of my belief and hope, the latter still are.

The story of my dialogues with Sati, my rescue lurcher, really begins in 2006. At the time I was with Karma, who was one of the loveliest characters I ever met. Another rescue dog, he was about three years old. A Comedy Dog – black and white, with a lovely head, longish ears, long body and tail and very, very short legs. There must have been basset in there somewhere. He attracted comments wherever we walked and delighted in absolutely all living creatures, bouncing enthusiastically up to any and all people and dogs.

Act One: Prologue

He had only two faults – he shed hair like mad and gloried in chasing cats. I don't think he wanted to harm them – it was just the thrill of the chase and a deep desire to play. But it made us unpopular in certain quarters.

Early in 2006, shortly after Karma and I moved into my present home, I had a bad bout of pneumonia. I was delirious for about a week (some of it was rather pleasant), then bed-bound for another three. Kindly neighbours who became friends used to take Karma for walks. He'd leave my side happily and bounce off with them, returning an hour or so later to thunder up the stairs and take a flying leap onto the bed, usually mud-covered and once having lost his collar in some rumpus. The neighbours were appalled: "Your bedcover!", but I didn't mind at all. I adored him.

Karma

Act One: Prologue

Sati:
(coming to my side)
So did you really love him, mummy?

Me:
Yes. Yes, I did. I do.

Sati:
More than me?

Me:
Umm – oh, you can't compare, darling.
You're my absolutely best boy now. OK?

Sati:
(slightly mollified)
OK, mummy.

He goes back to bed.

Act One: Prologue

In December 2006, I went to stay with friends in France, leaving Karma in the care of people we knew well – he'd been there before and got on famously with Zoe, their little fox terrier. (I wouldn't choose to put any dog, especially a rescue dog, in kennels – they've had enough of cages.)

December 8th. At midnight French time, I was in bed and dozing off. My mobile rang. I blearily answered it.

M: *Sara? Are you sitting down?*

Me: (instantly on guard) *In bed. Yes?*

M: (choked) *It's Karma. He was playing with Zoe this evening – they were both chasing that little ball they both love – you know – the yellow one with the bell inside. He somehow inhaled it – it got stuck in the back of his throat, and he suffocated. We took him straight to the vet's, but it was too late.*

Me: (robotic) *Suffocated?...Are...you...sure...he's...dead?*

M: *Yes – I'm so sorry. The vet said he was brain dead by the time he reached him. There was nothing we could do – we did try.*

Mechanically, I said all the right things – told him not to beat himself up, that it was an accident which couldn't have been foreseen; that he should ask the vet to put my dear boy in the freezer and that I'd see him when I got back. There was no point in catching the next flight home – the damage was done.

Act One: Prologue

We rang off, M still choked (he was so upset they sent him home from work the next day), and I proceeded to fall to pieces. I screamed (quietly), I hit my head against the wall, I madly scratched and bit myself. I went into the sitting room, found the whisky bottle, took an immense drink and collapsed sobbing on the floor in front of the dying fire. My friends heard me and came in and I somehow managed to tell them what had happened. They offered to drive me to the airport but I said it was pointless and I'd complete my stay. I still think I was right. I went through the rest of the holiday like an automaton and stayed that way for a very long time. I wanted to die too.

I questioned myself endlessly – would I have let it happen if I'd been there? Would I have realised that the little ball was a danger? Would I have kept a closer eye on the dogs and been quicker off the mark? We'll never know.

As soon as I got home, I bought some white roses (always significant for me – I don't know why), took another deep shot of whisky and asked Sheila, my dear landlady, if she would drive me to the vet's. I knew I couldn't have driven back, even if I managed to get myself there. (M is her son, so she was already involved.) Machine-like, I went into the vet's and asked to see my boy. They were a bit taken aback – they'd have liked longer to unfreeze him. I said it didn't matter. It didn't. They arranged him tastefully in a blanket, his little nose slightly squished from being against something else in the freezer. I cuddled his stiff body, kissed him and talked to him for a while. Then I put a rose between his paws and left him. We'd been together for just 20 months. I arranged for his cremation and to collect his ashes, and Sheila, also dripping tears, drove me home. Bless her.

Act One: Prologue

In the months that followed, I wasn't quite myself. The smell of all food became repellent to me. I barely ate. I lost two stone. People said I looked uncomfortably thin. I didn't notice – just registered dimly that my clothes were too big.

Well-meaning friends said I should get another dog as soon as possible. I couldn't do it. I got rid of all Karma's belongings – beds, toys, feeding bowls, the lot. I did visit the Dogs' Home a couple of times, once with a friend, but found I couldn't relate to any of the dozens of assorted and probably lovely dogs in there. My grief and, I guess, shock, were too deep to let me move on.

Three years passed. (They say you truly mourn a person for seven years, a dog for one. Untrue.) I kept Karma's ashes until the bluebells were in full bloom, then scattered them on his favourite walk. I know many people keep their pets' ashes at home, but I wanted him to go free. I felt no sense of release, though. But I started to eat again. I worked – I went up to the Lake District for eight months to do a theatre season. I looked after other people's dogs. I acquired a tenant with two small Jack Russell -Yorkshire terrier-type dogs. Hopeless. I couldn't relate to them, except with abstract kindness. (They were a handful too – I once had to collect one from the police station, after she got out – we'll never know how – and was found wandering on the High Street. She'd already lost one front leg from chasing cars.) I despatched my unwilling tenant.

Act One: Prologue

Sati comes in from the garden at this point, breathing heavily. He's been lying in the sun – he's an inveterate sun-worshipper, chasing patches of light all over the room. He would rather lie in the hottest spot, panting pathetically, than move to a perfectly good piece of shade two feet away. He comes to my left side and nudges me gently with his nose.

Sati:
How's it goin', mummy?

Me:
Oh – OK, darling. I'm working through the tough bits before you arrived. You know.

Sati:
(sagely)
I know.

Act One: Prologue

By the summer of 2009, I felt ready to give another dog a home. I went back to the Dogs' Home and met a boy who had been in there for quite some time, and badly needed permanent homing. A greyhound – as different from Karma as you could imagine. Beautiful, elegant, long legged – by no means a Comedy Dog. Taz. White with brown ears and a brown saddle. Gentle and sweet natured, as the breed tends to be. I visited him two or three times, then formally adopted him. They did tell me at the home that he could be aggressive with other dogs, and that I should always keep him muzzled if we were out, and not let him off the enormously long lead I bought from them.

We went home, where everything was prepared – two comfy beds, one by the radiator in the kitchen, one by the window in the bedroom. Toys, food, bowls, goodies, a warm coat.

He was absolutely lovely with all people – large and small, young and old, male and female. A delight. Maybe a bit hyper – always ready to leap up at the window to check any passers-by. Liked his own space sometimes. Not a snuggler. But beautiful. A joy at home.

His halo did occasionally slip – I had a friend from Canada staying with me, and was preparing supper one evening. You can't buy lamb in Canada, and she had a great fondness for it. So two exquisite lamb fillet steaks sat on the counter by the oven, lightly seasoned and garnished with tasteful sprigs of rosemary, ready to pop into the pan. I went into the sitting room to top up her drink and tell her that supper was imminent. Returning to the kitchen counter, I stopped in disbelief.

Act One: Prologue

The sprigs of rosemary were neatly in place. The lamb steaks had completely disappeared – vanished into thin air. Taz was exactly where I'd left him a minute earlier, sitting serenely on his comfy bed on the other side of the room. Looking, possibly, a bit smug. Short of spontaneous combustion, I came to the only possible conclusion.

Me: (appalled, but struggling not to laugh) *Oh, my lord – Taz has just eaten your supper!*

Consternation. He never owned up. It was the neatest job I'd ever seen – Fagin would have been proud of him. The boy could have made a fortune as a shop lifter.

Taz

Act One: Prologue

Sati:
(interrupting again)
So was he like me, mummy?

Me:
*Well...no, not really. He was bigger, for one thing.
A full-size greyhound...You know.*

Sati:
But was he LIKE me, mummy?

Me:
In some ways...but no. He was very scarred.

Sati:
I'M scarred, mummy.

Me:
*Yes, I know.
But not so much on the inside, I think.*

Sati:
(knowingly)
Ah. Yes. I see.

Act One: Prologue

I soon discovered that Taz's "can be aggressive with other dogs" was the understatement of the year. He literally saw red when he encountered another canine. He just wanted to hurl himself at them and attack. I don't know what had happened in his past, but it must have been very severe – he'd come from a home who gave him up because they said they were afraid of him biting their toddler.

Occasionally we'd pass another dog at a distance and Taz would walk calmly with supreme disdain. But usually he launched himself. He's a big, powerful boy. I walked him on a harness, so he wouldn't throttle himself, and the very long lead and always with the horrible muzzle, which he accepted like a lamb, as part of the going-out process. It felt a bit like accompanying Hannibal Lector.

But walking became a nightmare; in our town you can scarcely go outside onto the street without encountering at least one inoffensive pooch. After one particularly violent incident, my hands were bleeding, my fingertips swollen and going purple and I was very lucky not to have a broken finger or two. He'd never have turned on me, but he'd twisted so hard in his harness that he mangled my hands on several occasions.

Matters were exacerbated by the fact that Taz absolutely refused to relieve himself in any way in my little courtyard garden, which is mainly tarmac and pots, with one big flowerbed.

Act One: Prologue

After the first day or two, he recognised it as our territory and fastidiously refused to pollute it. I thought he might need grass (though after his long stay in the Dogs Home, I doubted it) and bought some turf, which I laid down in one corner, about 8 foot square. The first time he encountered it, he sniffed inquiringly and then did one small pee in a corner. Never again.

Through the wrought iron gate was my landlords' enormously long garden – this was fine, and they were extremely generous in letting us use it. But they also had a feisty, aggressive dog – Taz had hurled himself at her several times when they were on opposite sides of the gate. I used to wait anxiously until I was sure the family were out, then take him through. Glorious – it was the only time he ever ran free and without the horrible muzzle – the only occasions we experienced what I thought of as normal life for a dog. But I couldn't depend on using it; it wasn't a long term solution.

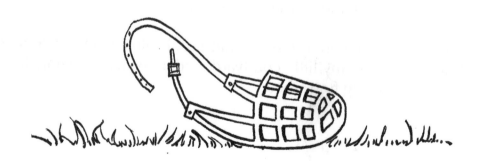

Act One: Prologue

We worked on Taz's Issue. I took him – at vast expense – to a homeopathic vet, deep in a remote part of the country. He'd already seen my vet of course, ("Yes, he's in splendid condition. A bit flat-footed, but no problems.") but I thought he might have a constitutional imbalance which could be corrected. Waste of time. We worked with strong, dog-expert friends. We worked with an animal behaviourist, who said confidently that she'd never yet met a dog she couldn't turn round, and he seemed a really lovely boy. Taz was, of course, angelic while we were at home. We took him out to a favourite dog walking spot, and she did her stuff ("Leave it! **LEAVE IT**!!"). She trained me too: "Keep relaxed. Don't let him know you're tense. Be confident – just walk him on." I knew all this and was quite good at it. But after a few weeks, we both admitted sadly that Taz was the first dog she couldn't turn round. He was unchanged.

After a couple of months, I was a physical and nervous wreck. I shook at the thought of taking him for walks. I paid people to do it for me. He wasn't quite so extreme with other people. At home, and with all human beings, he was delightful as ever. I agonised, but it became clear to me that I couldn't give him what he needed – either an immensely strong and thick-skinned handler, or a home where he didn't encounter other dogs

After eleven weeks of torture, I did what I could never have imagined myself doing. I called the Dogs' Home and asked them to take him back. Disappointed, they said yes, of course. I made a date.

Act One: Prologue

Sati:
(sadly)
Oh, mummy.

Me:
Yes, I know.
But it was an unbelievably bad situation.

Sati:
Hmmm.

I couldn't believe I'd done that. Several times I thought of calling back and saying I'd changed my mind. But the reality of our experiences, and the fact that I wasn't prepared to give up my whole life to go and live in an isolated cottage and just devote myself to looking after Taz, made me realise that this was the only viable solution. On his last night at home, I went to his bed, where he snuggled contentedly, knelt down and cuddled him. "I love you", I said. "I really love you. And I'm about to betray you. And you'll never understand."

Next morning Josie, a dog-expert friend who'd become very fond of Taz, asked if she could come with me. "Of course." I'd put all Taz's belongings in the car and written a long letter to the Dogs' Home, saying how lovely he was, what his well-being preferences were, and begging them to find a suitable home for him. (I'd already tried.)

I included a cheque for £500, which just about broke me, for his welfare/training. Taz came happily to the car, and we arrived at the Home he'd left just under three months before. He walked in confidently, and, as usual, greeted the care girl calmly and affectionately.

Act One: Prologue

It was only when we'd taken off his muzzle and he was put into the holding pen that he realised what had happened. His eyes rolled and he howled in protest – but went in like a lamb. It never occurred to him to turn and fight us. We left him, both of us crying. I delivered his goodies and the letter.

As we drove away, I choked out, "I can't believe I'm doing this". Josie said, "I'll never forget the look in his eyes when he went into that cage." I felt like Judas. A kiss, a betrayal.

I didn't go and hang myself from a tree, but I still ask myself if I could have done better by Taz. If only I'd been stronger, physically and emotionally. If only he'd shifted a bit. If only… .

For weeks I called the Dogs' Home to check on him. I was always told the same thing. He was still there; he was undergoing training. I was a bore, and taking up their time (unsaid). I was out of the picture. I never found out for sure what happened to him – another friend visited the Home and checked their website regularly, and one day he wasn't there. I only hope and pray he found the home he needed.

That was it. No more dogs, absolutely. I wasn't fit to have a dog. I didn't deserve one – that responsibility, that trust. Not for me.

The months passed.

Act Two: The Action

December 2009. I get a phone call out of the blue. It's Lynn, who knew Taz well and has become a good friend. She fosters greyhounds and lurchers for a local dog rescue charity, homing and socialising (and assessing) them until they get permanent owners. She's looked after a wide assortment of dogs, and is a bit of an angel.

Lynn: *Sara… could you do me a favour?*

Me: *Sure, anything…what?*

Lynn: *I've been asked to foster this dog…meant to be really nice. But Jonny (her partner) is being a bit funny. Says we've got one dog already and he doesn't want another one full-time. So would you help me foster him?*

Me: *Well…yes. But you know I haven't got any dog stuff left in the house. And I'm away next weekend…then for Christmas.*

Lynn: *Oh, that's OK. I'll take him then. Just not full-time. It's only till some-one adopts him. And he doesn't need much. I've got a big crate I can bring you – probably best if he sleeps in the kitchen till we know if he's housetrained. Just get some food in and find a couple of bowls and a blanket or two.*

Me: *Umm…. OK. Yes, of course. When?*

Lynn: *Wednesday? I can bring the crate over tomorrow.*

It's vast, and dominates the kitchen. I put a thick blanket in it, with a bowl of water and a dog chew.

.

Act Two: The Action

Wednesday evening. I've been working, so couldn't go with Lynn to pick up the dog. Scene: the kitchen – also the main entrance to my cottage. Door bell. I open the door.

Lynn: (cheerful) *Here we are. He's really nice.*

She is with a muddy brown dog – a bit smaller than a greyhound. He walks in, submissive without being humble, and stands patiently, waiting for inspection. Dull, rough coat. Half a dozen nasty-looking healing wounds (dog bites? barbed wire?), some of which have only just had the drains removed, and one perilously near his left eye. There is a small portion missing from the front of his tongue. His left ear is bitten through. Not emaciated, strictly speaking, but very thin. ("You could play a xylophone on those ribs!" Josie later remarks.) One foot is mangled and misshapen. He smells like a midden.

Me: (going down on my knees) *Let's have a look at you, sweetheart. Wow, you have been in the wars…God, he stinks!*

Lynn: (apologetic) *They always smell like that after they've been shipped over.*

He's come from Ireland, where he was rescued from a dog pound. I'm told there are more dogs abandoned in Ireland than in the rest of the UK put together, which when you consider the relative populations is pretty scary. We know nothing more about him – but later deduce that he may have been a gipsy dog and was used for hare coursing. One back foot is badly mangled, the toes twisted and swollen, the enormously long middle claw veering madly upwards and sideways at a right angle.

Act Two: The Action

Me: *It's fine – he just needs a bath.*

Lynn: *We'll give him one at the weekend.*

Me: *Come on, sweetheart. First things first.*

I give him a nourishing meal, which he eats enthusiastically. He smiles. So do I.

Me: *Does he have a name?*

Lynn: *They called him Tudor.*

Me: *Tudor? TUDOR? Sounds like a piece of furniture!*

Lynn: *You could call him Tod. Toddy.*

Me: *No, I know a Toddy. He's a killer Jack Russell who can turn on a sixpence and try to take your foot off. I guess he doesn't need a name right now. There are more important things.*

I was thinking of dogs' names weeks ago (why?) and thought I'd like to call my next dog (what next dog?) "Sati". Pronounced like Satin, without the "n". It's Pali (an extinct Indian language – I'm a Buddhist by now) and means "mindfulness". Short, sweet, could be male or female, and my dog reminds me to be mindful. Could this boy be Sati?

Lynn leaves and the dog and I settle down. I run my hands all over him, checking for other injuries or sore spots. None. We have a brief conversation.

Act Two: The Action

Me:
Sweetheart, I hope you're going to be OK here.

The Dog:
*Mmm. Better than my last place. Warm. People.
Food and water. Light. Cuddles.*

Me:
(warning)
It's just till you're properly adopted.

The Dog:
Mmm.

Me:
Well, bedtime. Come on. Last night pees and poos.

I lead the way into my little garden. He complies.
Back in the kitchen, I open the door to the crate.

Me:
In you go, sweetheart.

He walks in, docile. I close the door.

Me:
There you go. Comfy?

He lies down on the snuggly blanket.

Act Two: The Action

Me:
There's a drink and a chew. Sleep well.
I'll see you in the morning.

I turn off the lights and go upstairs. I've been in bed for about two minutes when I hear the sound of distress coming from the kitchen. The dog is crying. I know perfectly well what I should do. He's fine, and I should just leave him till the noise subsides and he falls asleep. No good. I can't do it. I turn on the lights and go downstairs.

Me:
Sweetheart – what's wrong?

The Dog:
(sobbing piteously)
Alone! ***ALONE!!***

I figure he's used to sleeping with other dogs. I'm stymied.

Me:
Oh, bugger! OK – but don't get used to it!
It's just for your first night.

The Dog:
Mmm.

I open the crate, take the snuggly blanket and lead the way upstairs. He follows, quiet and lamb-like. I arrange the blanket next to the radiator, near to my bed.

Act Two: The Action

Me:
(patting the blanket)
Here you go.

He slumps onto it, looking trustfully at me.

Me:
Just stay there. I'm right here. Sleep.

He does. I do. Peace.

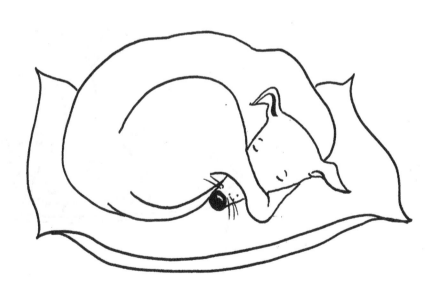

Act Two: The Action

I go off for the weekend and pick him up from Lynn. He is fine, He turns out to be a warm butterscotch colour, looks slightly fluffy and smells sweet, having been given the most wonderful bath – apparently he collapsed like a rag doll the moment the warm water hit him.

In the ensuing days, we grow closer. He never sleeps downstairs again, of course. He sleeps wherever he wants to. He has one comfy bed by the kitchen radiator, one in the bedroom, not far from mine. He has the choice of two sofas and a big armchair in the sitting room. (I've never subscribed to keeping dogs off the furniture – they're frequently cleaner than the people who sit there.)

Act Two: The Action

He always chooses to sleep close to me and, naturally, soon leaps onto my bed to snuggle beside me when he feels like it, luxuriously stretched out with his head on the other pillow. This can be rather uncomfortable – lurchers are angular dogs, and like to extend their legs. I often find myself occupying a precarious corner of the bed with Sati stretched out happily and horizontally on the rest.

Sati:
(reprovingly)
Mummy!

Me:
Well, you do. You know you do.

Sati:
Umm…yes. Suppose so.

He has a somewhat disconcerting habit. When happy and contented, his teeth chatter – a tiny movement, but very fast. When I first noticed this, I was concerned – was he cold? Frightened? But he was perfectly warm and relaxed, and it often happened when I was cuddling him, or when he was comfortably curled up. Karma used to smack his lips when he was happy – Sati sometimes does this too, but the chattering teeth is his trademark.

He really is the nicest person. He has just one fault – with 90% of other dogs, he's fine. With the other 10% he snarls, barks and lunges towards them aggressively. I'm reminded of my nightmares with Taz and shake. Perhaps this dog, too, isn't right for me – or me for him. I call the charity who own him, and say that I really like him and might adopt him – but could I have a bit more time, as I am concerned about his Dog Issue?

Act Two: The Action

I am told curtly that it's first come, first served as far as they are concerned – if I go away without committing myself, they'll give him to whoever is prepared to give him a home. Can I take the chance? Lynn has him for Christmas anyway, as I'm working on a cruise ship over Christmas and New Year, and obviously can't take a dog. I know I should stand firm – Lynn has told me, "They don't like taking adoptions over Christmas – it's too dodgy a time. People see the dog, like him, give him as a present, and he comes back in the New Year when they realise what looking after a dog really involves – they're not teddy bears." Can I risk it? I've grown very fond of him.

This breed are a breeze to look after, especially for a lazy person like myself. Elegant, long legged and built for speed, they've been described as "40 miles per hour couch potatoes".

They need relatively little exercise – one outing a day, usually involving some minutes of wild running, and they collapse for the next 24 hours. Spread elegantly, preferably across some soft furnishing, they can happily sleep/doze for 18 hours a day plus. Gorgeous. I realise how hyper dear Taz was in comparison.

I can't risk it. I call the charity and ask if I can officially adopt him. They say possibly, but I'll have to have a house check first. No problem – Lynn does house checks for them all the time. We pass with flying colours. He's mine.

Act Two: The Action

Me:
(reaching out to cuddle him)
Sati!

Sati:
Mummy! What's all the fuss about?

It's around this time that I realise I have been had, conned, set up. Lynn has always thought I should adopt another dog after Taz. She's fostered many dogs along with her own rescue lurcher, and her partner Jonny, far from ever being "funny" about it, is marvellously kind and generous with all dogs, and one of the best dog handlers I've ever had the privilege to meet. I fell for the scam – hook, line and sinker. But who cares? I have my boy.

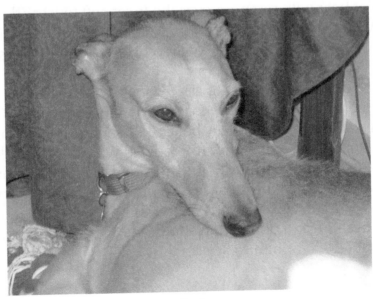

Sati

Act Two: The Action

Wilfred Nigel

I go away for my cruise, leaving Sati with his Christmas present - a squidgy polar bear with sewn-on eyes (he loves soft toys) and a pink furry thing for Wilfred Nigel, Lynn and Jonny's beautiful, pure white lurcher, who has become Sati's best chum. Wilfred likes pink. He's that sort of boy.

Lynn texts me on Christmas Day to say that Sati is having a great time, and has developed a fondness for smoked salmon and asparagus. Great – I'm a broke vegetarian. But I've never believed I should impose my choices on my dog, and I'll bet that if I confronted Sati with the ethical question of refusing to eat something from the meat industry or consuming a juicy steak, he'd go for the steak every time. Humans are omnivores. Dogs, as far as I can tell, were designed to be carnivores. So – he eats tinned and fresh meat. I don't. I have to hold my nose when I go into the butcher's, but I do it for him.

Act Two: The Action

Wilfred Nigel Painted by Lynn

I come back from my cruise and Sati and I have a joyful reunion - at least on my part. I think he's perfectly happy with Lynn and family, and doesn't really mind either way.

Act Two: The Action

We go to see my Splendid Vet (courtesy of Dodie Smith: 101 Dalmatians. He's never just the vet, always the Splendid Vet.) Sati has a thorough check up. He's already been neutered, wormed, vaccinated and identi-chipped by the charity. But I want him to have an MOT. The vet pronounces him in good shape – still too thin, but basically sound. Not great teeth; greyhounds and lurchers have notoriously bad teeth, unless they're really well looked after. One little front tooth is a blackened stump. The rest are more or less intact.

Me: *What about that foot?*

The vet looks closely at Sati's left hind paw.

Vet: *Hmm. Does it bother him much?*

Me: *Not really. He doesn't notice it most of the time. Sometimes he carries it when he's running – it must hurt. But that stray claw is something else.*

Vet: (inspecting it) *Yes…I can't trim it; the quick comes down all the way. I think the best thing to do is leave it for the moment – just keep an eye on it.*

Me: *So can you tell how old he is from his teeth?*

Vet: (chuckling) *No, you can only do that with rodents and ruminants. No idea. All I can tell you is that he isn't a very young dog or an old dog.*

Me: *Five?*

Vet: *Why not?*

We duly enter his birthday – five years before today's date on his records.

Act Two: The Action

The weeks pass. We grow closer. I train him to use the dog flap (this takes approximately 15 seconds), so he has 24-hour access to the garden and never has to wait with crossed paws until I decide to take him out. He trains me to give him only one meal a day (this takes a bit longer), by the simple expedient of totally ignoring his breakfast until about 4.30 in the afternoon. He gains weight. His coat thickens and becomes smooth and glossy. His wounds heal beautifully, though he'll always have scars. His eyes are bright. He's in good nick.

He now sleeps anywhere and everywhere, though favourite places remain his and my upstairs beds, and in a multitude of positions. On either side, sometimes curled into a neat ball, sometimes spread carelessly. Or flat on his back, rear legs akimbo, one front leg extended, the other relaxed, belly totally exposed – the picture of trust and abandonment. Sometimes in his utter relaxation, his nose squishes comically upwards – he looks just like a pig. He doesn't care; just snores a tad more loudly.

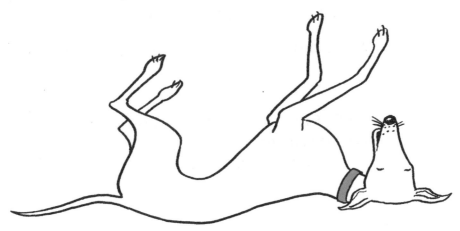

Act Two: The Action

There is the odd lavatorial lapse. One day I go into the guest bedroom, the door of which I have carelessly left ajar. At the bottom left hand corner of each twin bed is a large yellow stain, soaking the corner of the white bedspread and extending down to puddle on the pale green carpet. Perfect symmetry. I call him in:

Me:

Sati! What's THIS?

Sati:

(innocent)

Dunno, mummy. Can't imagine.

It's no good – I have no idea when the offence was committed. Chances are he's forgotten all about it. No point in reproaching him. But when I catch him in the act of cocking his leg against a floor-length curtain, I am very stern indeed.

Me:

NO! Grrr! STOP THAT!

Startled, he stops mid flow and looks round at me.

Me:

(furious)

NO! *Sati – that is SO unnecessary.*
You know you can go outside any time you want.
So what's this all about?

Act Two: The Action

Sati:
(subdued)
Dunno, mummy. Sorry. Just markin' my territory.

Me:
*Well, **DON'T!***

Once, I come back after a slightly-longer-than-usual outing to find a single enormous turd in the middle of the landing. A protest, I conclude. I call him to me, show it to him and express extreme disapproval. It never happens again.

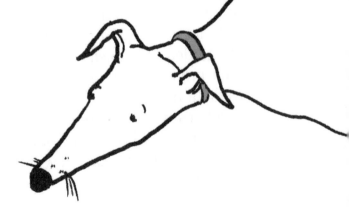

Act Two: The Action

Early Spring. The snow lies thick on the ground. With Frank and Sheila, my delightful landlords, I walk Sati in the empty fields with their dog, Penny. Sati loves the snow – he scoots along in it, nose down, like a hoover, often eating chunks of it.

Penny is a hugely furry girl – some kind of New Zealand sheepdog. She's also feisty, independent and often bloody-minded. She's bitten thirteen people so far, several on the face. She's lucky not to have been put down. Liking her freedom, she has become an escape artist and enjoys the odd night on the town. Their enormously long garden is securely walled on three sides, but at the bottom goes down to the river. Penny has worked out that if she asks to go out last thing at night, she can run the length of the garden, slip quietly into the river, swim next door and go up to the top of their property, where there is often an open gate onto the main road. Many a night she has spent on the streets, sometimes found outside the butcher's when he opens at 6.30am, begging for scraps, to be returned ignominiously home. I would be sick with worry if my dog disappeared overnight, but they bear it with fortitude – and her traffic sense does seem very good.

I am rather fond of her. When we first met, she accepted Karma after a few wary growls, but decided I was a total waste of space – just too boring to bother with. She was never aggressive; just stalked away with hauteur.

As the months passed she mellowed, finally deciding that I was the best thing since sliced bread. She used to whine at our dividing gate if I was in the garden, then hurl herself at me and flip onto her back to have her tummy tickled.

Act Two: The Action

Several times she barked pathetically at my kitchen door in the early morning, after one of her nights on the town. Several times I sighed, rescued her and delivered her home.

Once when Sati was staying overnight with friends and I'd been away working, I woke up in the morning and dimly registered that the dog in Sati's bed was the wrong colour. The bed was wringing wet...Penny had done one of her river trips and managed to get in through the dog flap. Too much of a lady to disturb my slumbers, she'd simply gone to sleep in Sati's bed. She looked at me steadily, perhaps just a fraction worried. I gave her some biscuits, took her home and put the bed in the washing machine.

This morning, walking with Frank and Sheila, Penny and Sati prance happily ahead, Penny sporting her usual fur, Sati in his warm, fleece-lined, waterproof coat. (This is not an affectation – lurchers have thinnish fur, very thin skin and practically no fat to insulate them from the cold. Without warm coats they tend to turn blue - yes, really - and shake.) It is a beautiful day, blue-skied and sunny, if freezing. The snow glistens, the river runs, deep and calm, on our left, with a couple of swans sailing elegantly on the water. We are thick in conversation.

Act Two: The Action

I suddenly realise that Penny continues to bounce in front, but Sati has disappeared. I look to my left. He is mid-stream, swimming hell for leather towards the swans a few yards ahead. I freeze, then shout in a voice whose volume and intensity surprises even me. Frank and Sheila stop dead in their tracks, mouths slightly agape. Even Penny is brought up short.

Me:
Sati! **NO!! SATI!! COME HERE!!**

Taken aback, he makes a right turn and swims towards the bank, increasingly hampered by the huge weight of water that has accumulated in the fleecy lining of his coat. Sinking slowly, he makes it to the edge and scrambles up, ending up in front of me. He looks up inquiringly.

Me:
(scolding furiously)
*You **STUPID** dog! Don't you know swans are dangerous?*
They can kill you if they turn on you. Idiot! You could have drowned!
Come here.

I remove the saturated coat.

Sati:
(as it slips over his head)
Er...I boobed, didn't I, mummy?

Me:
You certainly did!

I try to dry him off with my scarf and wring out the coat.

Act Two: The Action

Me:
I can't put it back on him – they'll both freeze.

Sheila:
Do you want to turn back?

Me:
No….he'll just have to keep moving.

I carry the sodden coat the rest of the way. Sati, his severe telling-off instantly forgotten, runs happily ahead. When we get back, I dry him off properly and put the coat in the washing machine. He is absolutely none the worse for his experience. I am weak with relief.

Act Two: The Action

The weeks pass. We settle down together. Sati's favourite pastime is, of course, dozing on a soft surface, which he happily does for many hours a day. I sometimes get curious.

The bedroom.
Sati sprawled out on his bed, eyes glazed.

Me:
Sati, what's going through your mind?

Sati:
Mmm...Oh, just thinkin' about
the Meaning of the Universe, mummy.
You know.

Me:
And have you come to any conclusions?

Sati:
Not exactly. Big subject. Got more thinkin' to do.
You know.

His eyes close completely, his cheeks blow out gently
as he starts snoring quietly.

Act Two: The Action

Sati having a nap

Act Two: The Action

"You know" is Sati's catch phrase. He uses it all the time: "Just (slurp) havin' a drink, mummy. You know." "Just havin' a stretch, mummy. You know" (he extends his front legs and angles forward all the way, then does the same backwards. He does this several times a day). "Just relaxin', mummy. You know."

You would expect him to have an Irish accent, as that is his provenance, but his voice is in fact slightly the genteel/off side of RP. (Received Pronunciation – the neutral "BBC voice".) We discuss this.

Me:
Sats?

Sati:
Mmm?

Me:
Why haven't you got an Irish accent?

Sati:
(opening one eye)
Dunno, mummy.

Me:
Mmm.

(He opens both eyes)

Act Two: The Action

Sati:
Although I AM Irish. You Know.

Me:
Yes, I know.

Sati thinks for a moment. Then, triumphantly:

Sati:
Begorrah, mummy!

Me:
(hiding a smile)
Yes, absolutely. Begorrah, Sats.

Sati
(dreamily)
Leprechauns an' stuff. Guinness.
You know.

He drifts back into slumber.

Act Two: The Action

His second favourite and time-consuming pastime is washing himself. Lurchers are wonderfully clean dogs by nature – they groom like cats. Sati assiduously washes his paws, running his tongue between his toes to dislodge any stray bits, his tummy, his legs, his bum (always spotless), any part he can reach. He quite often bites his legs and back to make quite sure. Favourite is willy-washing, which he performs with a series of loud gobbling and snuffling noises, as his nose gets squashed between his legs. He often does this during a quiet moment when we have guests. It can be a bit distracting. Luckily, the guests tend to be amused.

Me:
Blimey Sati – that's a bit graphic, old dear.

Sati:
(indistinctly)
Very important, mother – cleanliness.
A boy can't be too careful.
You know.

Act Two: The Action

Later, I bring a non-doggy friend home to visit. We enter by the kitchen door. Sati pads down the stairs to greet us. My friend approaches him, slightly gingerly. Sati just wags and then sits on his bed. My friend goes closer, patting him.

Friend: (in surprise) *He smells nice!*

Me: *Of course he smells nice. He lives with me!*

I once heard of a poor dog who thought his name was "Bed!" as he was told to go there so often. Sati probably thinks his name is "I love you". No – in fact he knows his name perfectly well. But when we are together, the air is thick with endearments. Nonsense names pop out from my lips without being filtered through my brain. Sats. Satirama. Mr Gorge. Caramel Cream. Monsieur Crème Brulee. Little Mister. Scrooble. Bright Eyes. Gorgeous Face. Mr Wicked. Boofulls. Sugar Pop. Mister Mister. Sausage Pot. Mr Fabuloso. Thunderpaws. Mr Bouncer. Sunbeam….the list is endless. Sati tolerates them all with a cheerful lack of discrimination.

As we progress into summer, it becomes clear that the dodgy foot is troubling him – he carries it increasingly and sometimes gives a little whine of pain. I take him to the Splendid Vet.

Me: *I'm really not happy about this foot – it gets painful. Is there anything you can do?*

Vet: (inspecting it closely) *Hmm. It's arthritis, of course, after the toes were damaged. Must be sore. And this claw really needs attending to now – it could catch on anything. Book him in – I'll do some x-rays and see what I can do. Take the claw off, I should think.*

Act Two: The Action

Me: (hopeful) *Will his Pet Insurance cover it?*

Vet: *Don't see why not. We'll give it a go.*

(In the event, the company refuses to pay a penny, saying that it was a pre-existing injury.)

At 8.00am a few days later I leave my dear boy to be anaesthetised and examined. I have guests staying with me, and am distracted the whole of the day. At 4.00pm the surgery nurse calls me to say I can collect him. I arrive; the Splendid Vet comes out to greet me.

Vet: *He's fine. Come into the office. Have a look at these.*

He projects several x-rays onto the wall.

Vet: *The good news is that his spine, hips and pelvis are absolutely clear – no sign of arthritis at all. But this foot.....all three front toes were broken. Probably stamped on by a horse, or a heavy boot. Never attended to, of course. So the toes have twisted and the joints spread. I was just going to take off the claw, but that wouldn't have worked. Then I thought I'd just whip off the first digit – but that would have left the upper one sticking out and vulnerable.*

In the end I took the whole middle toe off at the top. Much easier for him. The two outer toes are so broad there will scarcely be a space. Would you like to take him home?

Act Two: The Action

Five minutes and £550 later, I wait for Sati to come into reception.
I envisage a pathetic, limping creature with a huge bandage. (I imagine
how I'd feel if I'd had a toe amputated.)

Instead, he arrives cheerfully, stepping confidently towards me on all four
feet. There is a small dressing.

Me:
(Kneeling to embrace him)
Sats!

Sati:
Mummy! Hello….is it nearly supper time?

Mightily relieved, I take him home. He has some antibiotics, just in case.
The wound bleeds profusely if he walks on it too much, but is otherwise
fine. He is none the worse. I have some little white cotton ankle socks,
and learn to put one over the injured foot, securing it firmly but not tightly
with an elastic band halfway up his leg. I soon acquire a supply of white
cotton socks with brown stains at the toe, where the washing machine
didn't quite erase the blood. Over the next days and weeks, he recovers
fully. He never carries the foot or whines again. And the Splendid Vet
was absolutely right – the two outside toes are so spread that they leave
practically no gap in the middle.

Act Two: The Action

We resume proper walks. The cow fields just outside the town are one favourite. Today I check briefly that there are no looming cattle, and scramble over the gate, releasing Sati to climb under the bars. Turning on the other side I stop, horrified. Rabbits. The field is alive with them, peacefully grazing in the sunshine, or hopping gently to and fro. God….

Karma once caught a baby rabbit – I think more by luck than judgment. I don't believe he wanted to harm it in any way; it was just the thrill of the chase. He brought it back to me and laid it gently down in the soft grass beside the track, puzzled that it wouldn't play. We both inspected it. Its eyes rolled and it twitched all four limbs. It seemed to be completely uninjured – Karma had a very soft mouth – but I was afraid it would die of shock. Eventually we made sure it was in a soft and shaded place, and walked on. I felt awful. Probably Karma did too.

This is different. Like an arrow from a bow, Sati shoots forward towards the innocent grazers. I call him back – useless. Centuries of breeding and probably years of training are too hard to eradicate. One swoop. One pounce. One swift bite to the throat.

He comes towards me, proudly carrying the poor creature. It isn't a baby, but not quite full-grown. An adolescent, cut off in the springtime of its life. It is unmistakeably dead. I recoil, appalled.

Act Two: The Action

I should say at this point that I have a lamentable weakness. I can witness any amount of pain, physical or emotional, in a human being, and step in to help confidently and coolly. But the sight of any animal suffering – injured, abused, tortured, mutilated or dead – fills me with sick horror and grief. I genuinely mourn the creatures I see dead on the road – I once ran over a mink in Devon and went into shock. It's a serious neurosis and I should probably go and have some therapy. It would stand me in good stead now.

> Me:
> (backing off)
> *Urrgh! NO!! I mean* (I remember advice from another dog behaviourist) – *I mean well done, Sati. Good boy.*

He is only performing, supremely efficiently, what he was taught in his previous existence was his Function in Life. Who am I to condemn him?

> Me:
> *Er…yes. Good lad. Right. Now drop. Leave it. Leave it!*

He looks at me as if I'm demented. Drop? Leave it? His prize, his trophy, the evidence of his excellence? Never! He keeps a firm hold. I can't bear the thought of trying to prise it from his jaws – the prospect of the ensuing tussle is too awful. Besides, I couldn't touch it if you paid me. I don't know why; I'd happily hold a live rabbit, and this one was alive less than a minute ago.

I turn and apparently confidently, walk on – I hope he might see that I've lost interest and drop the poor creature. Not a bit of it.

Act Two: The Action

We walk the fields for the next twenty minutes, me trying at intervals to persuade him to abandon it and go and have some real fun, Sati firmly holding it aloft in triumph. I imagine the journey home – our walk up the crowded High Street, Sati proudly displaying his gory prize and me apologising to shocked and disapproving passers-by: "Yes, I know. I'm sorry. I'm really sorry. I just couldn't stop him." And what happens when we get home? Will he try to eat it? Will he expect me to eat it?? My thoughts run riot. I have a brainwave.

Me:
Sati, would you like to go in the river?

Sati:
Good idea, mummy!

Cheerfully, he agrees, dropping the rabbit carefully at the top of the bank as he descends to splash. I know what I should do at this point. I should quietly dispose of it – hide it, at least. No good. I can't touch it. I bring him out a little further down stream. Completely ignoring the rabbit, he accompanies me home.

Our walks are fraught with other difficulties. Sati, as I said, though absolutely fine and indeed positively friendly with 90% of dogs, has an active aversion to the other 10%. Conditioned by Taz, I develop a real fear of walking him down a crowded street by myself. On the surface, I handle the incidents quite well: "No! Leave it! Walk on. Just walk on. Don't be so silly," and I haul him onwards. He isn't nearly as violent as Taz, but pretty strong and determined. And it's impossible to predict which dogs are going to press his buttons.

Act Two: The Action

I go to a class in dog body-language, and talk to the trainer. He talks about dominant posture, eye contact, challenging behaviour. As far as I can see, none of this applies to Sati. He'll sound off at a perfectly innocent pooch walking on the other side of the road who, until Sati starts barking, hasn't even registered his presence. He's noticeably worse when he's with me, and on the lead.

"He's just trying to protect you," friends say fondly. I ain't convinced.

So many of our walks take place in my landlord's garden, which is huge and beautiful. A formal lawn with two enormous holly trees passes into a rose garden, then down past immensely long herbaceous borders to a little knot garden with herbs, over a rockery and into the orchard. At the end of this, the ground gets wilder and leads down to the river. Occasionally we startle a pheasant roosting in the undergrowth as we reach the nether regions of the property. It shrieks and takes off with all the lumbering effort of a jumbo jet, Sati leaping enthusiastically in pursuit. There have been a couple of near-misses, but happily no serious incident. We have an established routine, invented by Sati. At some point, usually in the afternoon (he's been in bed all day) I ask, "OK, do you want to bounce?" He invariably does – he leaps up and does a fair amount of preparatory bouncing as we go downstairs. He continues this as I prepare to go out, making it very hard to put on his coat in cold weather. We leave by the back door, I collect a poo bag or two and a couple of balls, and we go through the iron gate.

Act Two: The Action

Sati streaks through the formal garden – too boring to bother with – and makes his way to the orchard and the rough ground. He sniffs, pees, poos, munches grass, explores and potters around for about ten minutes, then suddenly turns and rushes up to me. This is my cue to throw the balls. He catches them dexterously in mid-air, then runs madly round the orchard with them, thundering along as if it's a race course.

Often he'll come to a screeching halt in front of the river bank (he really likes looking across the river at the field), and casually opens his mouth. The ball tumbles from between his jaws and slips gently into the river, floating downstream to be lost for ever. I buy quite a lot of balls. He rushes back to me, eagerly anticipating the next throw – his sense of cause and effect is poor. I bring out another ball – we never go out without at least two. I project the missiles for as long as he'll chase. At the next throw, he looks at me as if I'm mad and yawns gently, sometimes sitting firmly on the grass. A bit more pottering, sometimes a few reverse throws, and we make our way back, Sati occasionally stopping for a last pee on some unfortunate flower.

Act Two: The Action

Sati can pee for Britain. If it were an Olympic event, he'd probably have a gold medal. I never met a dog who could release so little so often. I once started to count how many pees he did on a walk, but gave up, bored, when I got to 25. He's also got the bladder control of a camel – he can last for 18 hours or more without bothering to go out. Enviable. Sometimes I feel guilty that I don't walk him in the outside world more often, but he seems perfectly happy and adequately exercised, his weight is a stable 24 kilos and the vet says he's in really good shape. We walk reasonably regularly with Lynn and her boys.

Boys. Another white lurcher has entered her life. Rough-coated this time. He looks a bit like a smallish Old English Sheepdog – lovely. Another fostering job – except when a perfectly nice couple arrived to see him, liked him and said they'd adopt him, Lynn dissolved into tears and realised she couldn't let him go.

So there he is – she initially called him Walter Gabriel, to go with Wilfred Nigel, but realised that it didn't really suit him, so he's become Douglas. Quite young. A bit hyper to start with – he's lived most of his previous life shut in a shed with no toys.Various skin conditions, and he screams if anyone touches his rear end. But totally without aggression – a bouncy, affectionate boy, keen on jumping up to lick your face (Sati is not a licker).

I am constantly amazed that these rescue dogs, many of whom have been treated appallingly by their former owners, remain so trusting and loving with all human beings.

Act Two: The Action

Unfortunately Sati decides that the thundering Douglas is simply Too Much – he becomes one of the hated 10%. Lynn asks if I'd mind muzzling Sati when we walk together or go to visit. I do – we both hate it, Sati trying pathetically to scratch it off at every opportunity. He stops staying there when I have to be away; Lynn couldn't risk leaving them together at night. Our life is impoverished.

But we work on it. Douglas starts calming down a little and gradually Sati stops reacting with aggression. On one walk, they both sniff at the same thing, heads together and tails wagging. Douglas sniffs Sati's rear end. Sati reciprocates. When we next visit, they are sharing a bed. They've become best chums – with the exception of Wilfred Nigel, of course. Douglas has a naughty habit of pinching Sati's treats – Sati is unworried about food and often doesn't eat them right away. Douglas wolfs his, then looks for more opportunities. If Sati is standing with a chew casually projecting from his mouth, Douglas coolly whips it out as he passes and demolishes it. Sati doesn't turn a hair.

Douglas

Act Two: The Action

Sati:
(coming up beside me as I write and determinedly
nudging me with his nose)
Mother?

Me:
(absorbed)
Mmm?

Sati:
(scraping his front paw excruciatingly down my left leg)
Look at me when I'm talkin' to you!

Me:
Ow! (rubbing my leg and turning to him)
Sorry.....what is it?

Sati:
I thought this book was called Dialogues with my Dog.

Me:
Yes, it is.

Sati:
Dialogues. Talkin'. You know.

Me:
Yes?

Sati:
There hasn't been much talkin' for AGES.

Act Two: The Action

I review the manuscript.

Me:
You know, you're absolutely right.
OK. What would you like to talk about?

Sati:
How about Dilys?

Me:
Dilys?

Sati:
Yes.
(meaningfully)
SHE was a handful, mummy.

Me:
(amused)
Yes, she certainly was.

Sati:
I liked her, though.
My ears have never been so clean.

Act Two: The Action

June 2012. I'm going with Caroline, a friend, to do some voluntary work in a local town – Sati is staying with Lynn for the afternoon. As I reach the main road, my attention is caught by a dog running free. A lurcher. Dirty, sandy colour. Very thin. No collar – but a cord deeply embedded in its neck, with a horrible looking wound all round, where the muscle has erupted over it. I ask about. No one has a clue. I run to Caroline's house – her husband Mike opens the door.

Me: *Mike, can I borrow Millie's lead? There's a dog on the loose, and I'm afraid it'll get run over.*

Mike instantly complies. Caroline comes to join me and we try to get the dog near enough to restrain it. No go. It comes forward a few steps, then skitters away again, running out of sight round the corner and down the crowded High Street.

Me: *Oh God – it'll get hit by a car! Hang on a sec.*

I rush into my kitchen and grab a couple of dog treats. We get into my car and follow the dog slowly down the High Street as it darts in and out of the traffic.

At the bottom, people are making slowing-down gestures. We pull up. The dog has paused on the pavement outside the Post Office to say hello to another dog that is tethered there. Caroline slips neatly out of the car, approaches the dog, goes down on her knees and talks softly to it, proffering the treats. Success. The dog reaches for them hungrily and Caroline gently slips the lead over its head, careful to avoid the wound.

Act Two: The Action

Graham, who owns the pet shop opposite and whose wife works for the Dogs' Home, comes over and offers to take it, saying he'll check it for an identity chip and give it a meal. It goes off with him like a lamb. We continue our afternoon's work. When I collect Sati that evening, I tell Lynn the story.

Lynn: (instantly alert) *Might be a gipsy dog – either kicked out or broken free. What's going to happen to it?*

Me: *I've really no idea. Hopefully the Dogs' Home will take it in. Or maybe your charity would.*

Lynn, Champion of Lost Lurchers, is not satisfied with this. Next morning she goes to the pet shop and makes enquiries. Of course, the dog had no identity chip – it remains a mystery.

The Dogs' Home, though quite near, is technically in the next county, and won't take her. Ditto Lynn's charity. The dog is sent to the local pound where, if not claimed within seven days, she may have to be put down.

Lynn's eyes fill with tears.

Lynn: *She's only young...about ten months. And healthy. And really nice.*

She finally sweet-talks her charity into taking on the dog – with the proviso that Lynn fosters her until a suitable home can be found. She goes to their vet, where her neck wound is treated (it heals perfectly) and she is vaccinated and wormed – she's a tad young to be neutered.

Act Two: The Action

She arrives at Lynn's. After a bath it emerges that she, too, is pure white. Lynn calls her Dilys Maude (Lynn's dogs' names often have an Edwardian ring to them). She is, as Sati remarked, a Bit of a Handful. Young, bouncy, enthusiastic and having the time of her life in a loving home with two other dogs. She sleeps peacefully in Lynn's crate, so she doesn't drive Wilfred and Douglas mad all night. Puppy-like, she demolishes various household objects. Cushions and tables lose their corners. Lynn calls me up:

Lynn: *I'm on the land line…Dilys has just eaten my mobile phone!*

When we visit them and Sati is introduced to her, astonishingly he takes to her at once. He finds her a bit much, but is always benevolent. She loves him, washing him assiduously. But it means he can't stay there while I'm away – Lynn can just about cope with exercising three dogs, but not four.

We search for alternative accommodation when I have to go away and meet Jackie, who lives locally in a lovely home with a spectacularly large garden and whose business is dog walking and hospitality. She has her own spaniel, Baloo, who takes to Sati at once, though he seldom bothers with other dogs. Sati likes him, too. I tell Jackie about his problem with 10% of dogs. She is hugely professional and kind, and an energetic and indefatigable dog walker. She is confident – and indeed, every time he goes to stay overnight with an assortment of other dogs, she says he's been fabulous and that all the others really take to him. Phew. So is it just me?

Act Two: The Action

Me:
Sati?

Sati:
(Lazily opening one eye)
Yes, mummy?

Me:
Is it just me?

Sati:
(yawning)
No, mummy.
I sometimes do it when you're not there, too.

Me:
(semi-relieved)
Ah.

Sati:
(grinning)
Just not as bad, mummy. You know.

He goes back to sleep.

Dilys is adopted by a friendly couple about four months later, having met their other dog. Lynn's eyes fill with tears, but she lets her go.

Act Two: The Action

Sati and I do have Incidents.

3 am. The bedroom. We are both deeply asleep – Sati on his bed, me in mine. A sound, undetectable to the human ear, floats up from the garden. In a fraction of a second, Sati is fully alert, on his feet and barking madly.

Sati:
INTRUDER! INTRUDER!! INTRUDER!!!

He sounds a bit like a Dalek, but, alas, far louder and much more mobile.

Me:
(struggling to surface)
Sati….What the...?

He zooms over to the side window, whose sill is at floor level. Parting the curtains with his nose, he carelessly kicks aside my Wireless Router and two rather fragile glass bottles, one of which breaks. He stares urgently out at the garden, still barking madly, then thunders downstairs. I hear the dog flap swing. The barking continues as he alerts the emergency services.

A bit alarmed, I sleepily slip on a pair of shoes and follow him out.

Me:
What on earth…?

Sati stands stiffly, ears pricked, tail high and moving in wide sweeps (I've done my dog body language class), the image of the Noble Beast poised to defend his nearest and dearest.

Act Two: The Action

Sati:
CAT/FOX! CAT/FOX! CAT/FOX!

All – except Sati – is quiet and still.

Me:
(wearily)
Oh, REALLY Sati! If there ever was anything, it's long gone. Stop it.
Come on – come upstairs. Come ON!

Reluctantly, he follows me, continuing to pace the bedroom for several minutes before resuming his slumbers. It takes me ages to get back to sleep – I'm quite shaken. I enviously listen to him snoring gently.

This Event is repeated the following night. And the next. And the next. Always at about 3 am. I take to placing a chair in front of the window so he can't stand on the sill. This is only a slight deterrent. I cease to accompany him downstairs, finally confining myself to swearing sleepily and shoving my head under the pillow. I'm waiting for complaints from the neighbours. (There are none.) After several more nights, it stops. Perhaps the possible visiting fox decided it was too much hassle.

Act Two: The Action

Another low moment: I am having lunch with friends in a local town; Sati is invited too. It is a lovely day and they have a large, dog-proof garden, so the French windows are open and he comes in and out. A group of eight of us are just finishing the main course, chattering like monkeys. The son of the house suddenly looks behind him at something on the carpet.

Jake: *OMIGOD! He's got a bird.*

Sati is standing quietly, waiting for praise, but too well-mannered to intrude on the conversation. Beside him on the floor is a large blackbird. It looks in the prime of life and in peak condition. Unfortunately it is dead. General consternation and, not least from me, repulsion.

Sue: (sadly) *Ah yes, I know that bird. He used to come down for crumbs.*

I feel terrible. Another life cut short – and it's all our fault. I know it's my responsibility to deal with this, and try to fight my horror.

Luckily Claire, who is supremely cool-headed and sensible, rescues me. She gets up, grabs a handful of paper towels, calmly sweeps the bird up and disposes of it responsibly in the bin outside.

Me: (shaky)….*It was really dead?*

Claire: (brisk) *Oh, yes. Right – that's over. Shall we get on with pudding?*

Me: *Yes…I am SO sorry, everyone. I'm mortified. And Sati, so should you be!*

He stands, a little sad, deprived of praise for his skill and swiftness.

Act Two: The Action

Me:
Oh – come here.

He does.

Me:
(stroking the miscreant)
Yes, I know….centuries of breeding ….

Sati:
…and years of training…you know, mummy. I was clever though, wasn't I?

Me:
(sighing)
Yes. Yes, you were.

Sati:
*It's **What Dogs Do**, mummy. You know.*

Me:
I know.

Although he likes most dogs, Sati is essentially a people person – he seems genuinely unhappy if left alone for too long. My house rule is that he's never left for more than four hours at a stretch. This limits my social life somewhat. Sati greets all people with delight, shamelessly playing the field if there are several present. My Canadian friend returns, to run a series of advanced workshops for senior acupuncture practitioners, some in my sitting room. It can just about hold ten people in comfort. They duly arrive and I check whether anyone is allergic to or dislikes dogs. No; they all really LIKE dogs. So Sati is allowed to participate.

Act Two: The Action

He's always calm and gentle, never jumps up or barks (except occasionally with me), so all is well. I go in just before the end of the morning session to check that everyone is OK. Two of the practitioners are sitting on the floor, books propped uncomfortably in front of them. Sati is cheerfully occupying a seat-and-a-half on the sofa, snuggling up to another student and looking as though he understands every word.

Me:
(shocked)
Sati – that is OUTRAGEOUS!

Sati:
(innocent)
What, mummy? I was invited. You know.

Me:
(incredulous)
Is that true? Are you really OK with this, guys?

I am told that it is and they are.

Me:
*Sati, wouldn't you like to come upstairs and
keep me company? Sweetheart?*

Sati:
No, mummy. More people here. More cuddles. You know.

Me:
(as I leave, defeated)
Tart!

Act Two: The Action

He needs multiple cuddles much of the time – except, of course when asleep, which is a lot. If I approach him then, kissing his head and asking if he's all right, he buries his nose between his paws so deep his eyes are covered.

Sati:
(muffled)
I'm not here, mummy. You can SEE that. I'm incommunicado.

But I am not allowed to respond in kind. I have an unfortunate enthusiasm for playing Internet Scrabble and always have about a dozen games on the go with friends in various parts of the world. I get very absorbed.

Afternoon. Sati has been asleep on my bed for hours. I am mid-game. He comes quietly up to my left side. I don't notice. He gently touches me with the side of his head.

Sati:
Mummy?

Me:
Mmm? Oh, hello, darling.
I absent-mindedly run my hand down his back.

Sati:
Mummy!

He gives me a definite nudge with his nose.

Me:
Mmm...... with you in a minute, love.

Act Two: The Action

Sati:
MUMMY!

He runs his right front paw, steel-tipped, all the way down my leg.

Me:
Oww! Sati, that really hurts!

Sati:
It's not good enough, mother. Here I AM. You know.

Me:
(sighing and abandoning the game)
Yes, I know. I'm sorry.

I cuddle him extravagantly for several minutes.

Me:
There. Is that enough now?

I go back to my game.
He comes round to my right side and repeats the nudging process.

Sati:
Frankly, no, mummy, it's not. More….please.

After several more minutes' stroking, kissing and tickling,
he subsides, temporarily contented.

Act Two: The Action

He also seems contented with the way he looks when we go out. I am not so sure. His old green waterproof coat – a hand-me-down from one of Lynn's former dogs – is serviceable, but hardly smart. At an online auction for an animal charity, I bid for what is described as a luxurious coat, and a truly splendid custom-made hound's collar. To my amazement, I get them both. The collar is astonishing – wide, gold and scarlet, with an optional fob of pretend rubies. We ditch the fob right away – it clonks him under the chin when he runs. The collar we keep for party wear, but seldom remember to put it on.

The coat arrives – a resplendent garment. Beautifully warm and soft, it is hand-made from pure Scottish wool in tiny red and bright blue checks, with a dark blue velvet trim round the whole thing, and a little medal stating its provenance.

Me:
Cor, Sats, that's amazing!

Sati:
Er…..yes, mummy.

Me:
(enthusiastic)
Let's try it on!

It fits perfectly front to back, but is a tad long. A lovely thing, though. We keep it for very cold, dry days and Sati tears about in it, valiantly trying to ignore the slight encumbrance round the tops of his legs. After two or three outings, I face the facts.

68

Act Two: The Action

Me:
It's no good, sugar-pop. It's just not you.

Sati:
(subdued)
Yes, mummy. I know.

Brown and scarred as he is, the startling brightness of the coat looks...wrong. It's just too smart, and he really needs autumn colours. The excessive length makes him look slightly unbalanced.

Me:
Sats darling...... you look like a horse in a medieval pageant.
Shall we go back to your old green one? It's perfectly fine.

Sati:
Oh, yes PLEASE, mummy!

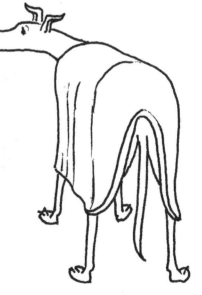

Me:
It's no good, old love.
We weren't meant to look Resplendent.
We're more the casual type.

Sati:
I know.
It's not as if I'm a Pedigree Dog.

Me:
(fervently)
Thank heaven!

Act Two: The Action

I've nothing against pedigree dogs as such, but I do have serious misgivings when I look at some of the results of over-breeding. Poor animals bred to have squashed faces, so their breathing tubes are restricted. Ears so long they constantly get infections. Hip dysplasia. Skin Sensitivity. Neuroses.

We sometimes walk with a delightful English bulldog called Daisy, who is constantly at the vet's with various unnecessary ailments. In particular, her poor feet are so sensitive it really hurts her to walk on hard surfaces. Give me a happy, healthy, balanced, unique crossbreed any day. It seems madness to breed animals with potential problems, just to conform to some mythical Breed Standard dreamed up by someone who isn't even a dog.

We donate the glamorous garment to Wilfred Nigel who, being pure white and a tad taller than Sati, looks magnificent in it, and attracts admiring comments every time he walks out.

Sati: Fashion mistake

Wilfred: A triumph

Act Two: The Action

I meditate every day, and Sati respects that – he once started to nudge my shoulder gently with his nose, but receiving absolutely no response, wisely decided that at these moments I too was incommunicado. But sometimes he interrupts my studying. I am absorbed, frowning slightly. Sati comes up to my side and introduces himself with an extended paw.

Sati:
Mummy – what's that?

Me:
*Mmph? Oh – it's The Drama of Cosmic Enlightenment
– the Lotus Sutra.*

Sati:
(impressed)
Cor! So what's THAT when it's at home?

Me:
*Er…it's hard to explain. Give me a bit of time;
I've only just started reading.*

Sati:
(sceptical)
Huh! Well, perhaps you'll let me know, mother, when you find out.

Dignified, he slopes off to his bed, where he lies with eyes glazed for several minutes before closing them completely.

I am a bit of a night bird, often so absorbed in what I'm doing (frequently Scrabble) that I'm still about at 2 or 3am. I also do some overnight shifts for a large charity in a local town.

Act Two: The Action

Sati accompanies me on these trips, snoozing in a comfy chair covered in a huge towel, while I man my telephone/computer. At the end of a shift, I rouse him:

Me:
Sati! 7 o'clock. Home time. Come on.

Nothing. I show him his lead and/or coat.

Me:
Sati! Come ON!

Nothing.

Me:
(exasperated)
Sati! WILL you get your bum off that chair?
Come on, darling; I'm exhausted. Home to proper bed.

Sati yawns hugely, immobile.
My colleagues on the next shift look on, amused.

Me:
SATI!

I try to lift the towel off the back of the chair,
to dislodge his bum. Eventually:

Sati:
(with dignity)
I AM comin', of course, mother.
But…in…my…own…time.

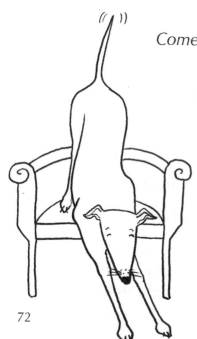

Act Two: The Action

Slowly, he extends his front legs onto the floor. He leans forward onto them, stretching the whole of his back and legs. His rear paws finally slip to the ground. He ambles towards me and we venture forth into the dawn.

So our body clocks aren't altogether synchronised. Occasionally he will wake in the middle of the night and decide it's play time. He usually contents himself with a quick visit to the garden and breaking the necks of a soft toy or two, while I sleep on.

Sometimes he's not contented with this – he wants some real action. Digging purposefully down through the archeological layers of his toy box, he finds what he's looking for at the very bottom. His one and only loud, squeaky toy – a gift, and not from me. Pouncing on it with delight, he attacks it enthusiastically. Hurling it in the air and catching it, he thunders round the bedroom with it, biting with force. It squeaks ear-splittingly in protest. I am dredged up from the depths of some dark dream.

Me:
(groaning)
Gawd, Sat...that's awful.

Sati:
Good, isn't it mummy? Wheee!

I shove the pillows over my head
and pray for oblivion.

SQUEAK!

Act Two: The Action

Time for Sati's annual check with the Splendid Vet, who pronounces him in fine fettle, but is concerned about his teeth.

Vet: *You can see there's quite a bit of gum inflammation here at the back… we don't want him to lose those teeth or get an infection. They really need professionally cleaning and scraping. And I'm not sure about this little black one at the front.*

Me: *That means knocking him out, doesn't it?*

Vet: (cheerful) *Oh, yes. It's a day procedure.*

Me: (with trepidation) *So how much is it likely to cost?*

Vet: (still cheerful) *Oh, upwards of two hundred and fifty pounds.*

I am utterly broke – work has been very scarce lately.

Me: *I suppose his Pet Insurance won't cover it?*

Vet: *No, I'm afraid they never cover dental work.*

I gulp, then arrange Sati's appointment. Some things are more important than money.

Subsequently, I tell another friend in the local town about this. She is shocked – and 30 years ago she lost a beloved dog, a Pug, through gum disease. It wasn't diagnosed so efficiently then, and it had progressed so far that the dog's jaw broke; the bone had become so porous that it couldn't be repaired or wired up. The dog had to be put down. She never got over this.

Act Two: The Action

With huge generosity, she says that OF COURSE Sati must have the treatment, and transfers £250 into my bank account to pay for it. I remain hugely grateful.

On the appointed day, I deposit Sati in the morning and get a call at tea-time saying I can pick him up. He's had a thorough clean and scrape, and the little dead tooth at the front removed. He is a sad and sorry boy – he's still woozy, has blood on his muzzle and is crying. Seeing me, he makes a pathetically inefficient attempt to climb onto the narrow wooden bench beside me.

Sati:
Mummy... Where WERE you?

Me:
(cuddling)
I'm sorry, darling.

Sati:
They HURT me, mummy…It hurts.

Me:
I know. It's all right. We're off home now.

Back at the house, he is still miserable, giving little distressed whines and slumping onto his kitchen bed. After an hour of this, I call Lynn for advice.

Me: *He's obviously in pain. Is there anything I can give him?*

How different from the toe amputation, when he bounced home happily!

Lynn: *You could try aspirin, he's probably still getting over the anaesthetic.*

Act Two: The Action

I pop over the road, where I buy the mildest aspirin they sell. I break a pill in half and dissolve it in warm milk – a treat; he hardly ever gets to drink milk. A solid supper is obviously out of the question. He slurps it. An hour or so later, the whining stops and he becomes perkier.

Next day he is back to normal, though we still have soft food for a day or two. His teeth are spectacularly clean.

I start adding a seaweed-based product to his supper – it claims to keep plaque at bay. Who knows? It's worth a try. He also has a daily supplement of Glucosamine, in case the dodgy foot gets more arthritic. It's meant to be a delicious chicken-flavoured treat. He spurns it utterly, so I crush it into his food. A dribble of cod liver oil completes the medication. He also has some charcoal biscuits daily, to aid digestion and neutralise any unpleasant odours which might emerge from his rear end. Again, he spurns these – just too boring to bother eating, so they too get crushed. He then has half a tin of good quality dog meat and some fresh meat daily – usually raw liver. As a vegetarian, I find his meals less than appetising to prepare. I put on rubber gloves and cut up the horrible, slimy, blood-dripping slices of liver with kitchen scissors; lucky he's trained me to give him only one meal a day. A mug of dry food completes the feast. His supper often takes longer to prepare than mine.

Act Two: The Action

Sometimes he dreams – the eye-rolling, twitching, rabbit-chasing movements which most dogs make. Occasionally it's different – he lets forth a series of pitiful little whimpers and seems distressed. I kneel down beside him.

Me:
Sats….Sati darling. You're dreaming.

I slowly stroke him. He semi-rouses.

Me:
Sweetheart, you're dreaming. It's just a dream.

Sati:
(indistinctly)
Bad stuff…

Me:
*I know. But you're safe here with your mummy.
You're safe. Come here.*

Gently I cuddle him; he subsides.

Sati:
(still half asleep)
Mmm…better, mummy.

Me:
Good.

Sati:
Mmm.

He snores gently.

Act Two: The Action

He regularly customises the sofas in the sitting room. Digging vigorously, he reshapes them to his personal taste. Cushions fly all over the room, propelled by his nose. The throw protecting the pale cream upholstery (bought before I acquired him) lies in a wrinkled heap on the floor. I automatically check whether the place is habitable before we have any visitors. Then one day he's given some rather unpleasant white chewy things as treats – based on pig hide, I fear. He loves these, taking them firmly to the dark green sofa to munch them. The sofa is soon covered with white gooey stains. Impossible to brush or sponge off. I decide that I have nothing to lose by putting the seat covers through the washing machine. I do. Success. Reluctant to put the covers in the dryer, in case they shrink, I hang them over a radiator overnight. I thoughtlessly go to bed. In the morning I wander into the sitting room. It is full of snow. Sati has done his usual digging/nesting exercise on the sofa and scratched straight through the delicate inner covers. Delighted with his find, he has invented a wonderful game of digging out the seat stuffing with his nose and depositing it all over the room.

Act Two: The Action

Me:
SATI!   What's THIS??

Sati:
(arriving)
What mummy?

Me:
What do you mean, WHAT? Look at this place!

Sati:
Ah. Yes.
(grinning hopefully)
Fun, isn't it, mummy?

Me:
FUN??

It's no good. I can't keep up the righteous indignation. The sight is too absurd. Reluctantly, I start grinning too.

Me:
Fun for you, perhaps. Work for me!

I laboriously gather up the stuffing and ram it all back into the gaping hole, sew it up and replace the cushion covers. No one would ever know.

Act Two: The Action

We have a number of routines/rituals, mainly invented by Sati. Bed time is the most firm. Although he can go out to relieve himself at any time, I think it's a good idea to visit the garden just before we go to bed. At some time between 11pm and 3am, when he is usually zonked out on one of our beds, I leave the computer or whatever, stretch and lead the way downstairs.

Me:
Come on, Sats. Pees and poos.

Nothing.

Me:
Sati! Pees and poos. Come on, lovely.

Still nothing. I go downstairs to the kitchen.

Me:
Sati! Come on!

Nothing again.

Me:
OK, it's totally up to you. But you won't get your treats.

A pause, then a pointy nose and two ears, often facing in different directions, appear through the bannisters.

Sati:
Here I am, mummy.

Me:
Good lad. Come on.

Act Two: The Action

I lead the way to the garden, Sati inspecting his supper bowl and occasionally eating any remnants before following. I open the sitting room door.

Me:
Out we go!

He follows, wanders into the garden and usually produces an enormous and long lasting fountain - the only time he pees in one go.

Me:
Good lad. In we go.
He follows me into the kitchen.

Me:
What do we have now?

Sati:
(enthusiastically)
Delicious chew, mummy!

Me:
Yes! Here you are.

He munches it. I do the odd clearing up job.

Me:
And what next?

Sati:
(obediently)
Delicious Joint Stick, mummy.

Me:
Yes! Here we go.

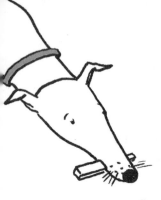

Act Two: The Action

He munches it – full (it claims) of joint-supporting goodies, while I finish tidying.

Me:
And what do we have when we go to bed?

Sati:
(mechanically)
Dental Stick, mummy.

I like him to end his day with one of these – they are supposed to keep his teeth clean. I proffer it. He totally ignores it.

Me:
Come on, then. Up we go.

I turn out the lights and make for the staircase. He picks up the dental stick and precedes me, holding it sideways in his mouth. Lurchers usually move with an elegant flow. Going up or down stairs is different. If you follow one, you'll see that they walk like ducks, their rear ends swaying comically from side to side as they shift weight. It's a bit like following an old gentleman with a large cigar. Winston Churchill, perhaps, or Orson Welles.

We reach the bedroom, where he usually sits firmly on the rug between our beds and consumes it.

Sometimes he doesn't bother. He stock piles the sticks on the bedroom floor for several days – I tread on them in bare feet and wince, then gather them up, squirrel them downstairs and produce one triumphantly again the next night. He indulges me in this.

Act Two: The Action

He tends to start the night in his own bed and end up in mine. Often I wake to find a pointy nose facing me, his head on the other pillow and sometimes his paws round my neck. Sometimes he curls up and presents his bum.

Occasionally, my sleep is rudely broken. He jumps gently onto the bed beside me and we both sleep, facing each other. At some point in the night, one sharp-clawed front paw will shoot straight forward like a thrust bayonet, implanting itself firmly in my breast. I scream and wake.

Me:
Oh.....Sati! OWW! That is AGONY!

Sati:
(still mostly asleep)
Mmm. Sorry, mummy.

Impermanence is a major Buddhist theme, and living with a beloved animal brings home the universal truth of it with ultimate force. I never take our life together for granted. The life-span of a lurcher is...what? Twelve, maybe? I don't really know how old he is - if he was five when I got him, he must be at least eight by now. And I don't know what his previous life was like, except that it must have been grim. Lynn remarks that she thinks he's going white around his muzzle. And we never know what accidents or diseases may wait around the corner. Every day I say to myself: "This is temporary. This is not forever," and I know that when I lose him, I'll be devastated. I remember a fragment of a poem I once read:

...Beware!
Never give your heart to a dog to tear.

Act Two: The Action

But what do you do? Make a conscious choice not to love, as one friend of mine has done, and forego the joy as well as the inevitable suffering? I have no answers. I just know that we have to make the most of each day together.

So, are my dogs surrogate children? I sometimes ask myself this (no one else has been tactless enough to suggest it), and I really don't think so.

I've always had an instinctive love and respect for animals and tend to relate to them as equals. I don't see why human beings should assume superiority just because we've developed the kind of brain that is "self-conscious", can use tools, invent the wheel and harness fire. All this can lead to some pretty disastrous stuff – we're the only species likely to extinguish ourselves (and a lot of others) actively. Is that true intelligence? How dare we assume that animals' intelligence is inferior, because they don't speak with our language or use computers?

Consider migrating birds or salmon, the social structures of ants and bees… The efficacy of their communication and the complexity of their behaviour is mind-blowing. There is more in heaven and earth, Horatio (sorry – I had to slip in one Shakespearean quote).

Sati:
Blimey, that's a bit philosophical, mater.

Me:
Mmm, it is a bit, isn't it? Perhaps I should leave it right there.

Sati:
(dryly)
I would, mummy.

Finale

Bed time again. The bedroom. Sati is comfortably stretched out in his bed, on his tummy, front legs outstretched and nose pushed between them.

Me:
Sati?

Sati:
Mmm?

I sit on my bed and pat it invitingly.

Me:
Would you like to come and sleep with me? Sats?

Sati:
(firmly)
No thank you, mummy.

Me:
Oh, OK.

I sigh, switch off the light and turn on my side, away from him. In the middle of the night, I am peacefully unconscious when I become aware of a cold pointy nose nuzzling into my neck.

Sati:
(muffled)
Mummy?

Me:
(mostly asleep)
Mmm? What, darling?

Finale

Sati:
I'm feelin' a bit alone.
Can I have a cuddle?

Me:
Sure, sweetheart. Come here.

I kiss his nose and blow warm air on to the velvet-soft top of his head, putting one arm round him to keep him close and snuggle him.

He goes back to sleep. So do I.

Peace.

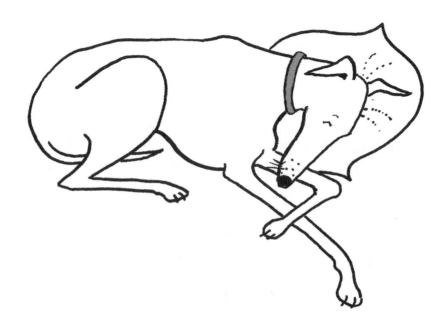

Curtain Call

Mid afternoon.
I leave the computer, stretch and go to sit beside Sati.

Me:
That's it darling. It's done.
Your book: Dialogues with my Dog.
Thank you for all your contributions.

Sati:
I'm glad you're pleased, mummy.
Will you have more time to play with me now?

Me:
Yes lovely boy.
You've been very patient while I was writing our story.

Sati:
Will you read it to me?

Me:
Of course I shall.

Sati:
Cor! Will I like it?

Me:
I hope so. It's all about you.

Sati:
So will lots of people read it, mummy?
Will I be famous?

Curtain Call

Me:
*Dunno. I doubt it. It's not exactly bestseller material –
it's not about to take the literary world by storm.*

Sati:
(momentarily crestfallen)
Oh. Still
(brightening),
*that's not really important, is it mummy?
You know.*

Me:
(smiling back)
You know, Sats – it's really not.

Cast

Sara Coward and her rescue lurcher, Sati, live together
in a small town in Warwickshire.

Sara is best known to Radio 4 listeners as the voice of Caroline in The Archers.
She also appears regularly on stage, does after-dinner entertainments,
records audio books and makes occasional forays into TV.

Sati has no gainful employment, but is worth his weight in gold.

Ali Wylie lives in a small village outside of Stratford-upon-Avon.

Ali has had a life-long love of dogs of all shapes, sizes and personalities.
Her admiration for their loyalty, bravery and optimistic outlook on life
is captured and reflected in her illustrations.

She is a volunteer for the charities
'Dogs for the Disabled' and 'The Dogs Trust'.

Cover photography: Roy Peters

Lightning Source UK Ltd.
Milton Keynes UK
UKOW06f1235281113

222017UK00001B/1/P